# Elaine Lustig Cohen
## Modernism Reimagined

BY AARIS SHERIN

# LUSTIG COHEN

## Elaine Lustig Cohen
## Modernism Reimagined

BY AARIS SHERIN

GRAPHIC DESIGN ARCHIVES
CHAPBOOK SERIES: FIVE

RIT PRESS
2014

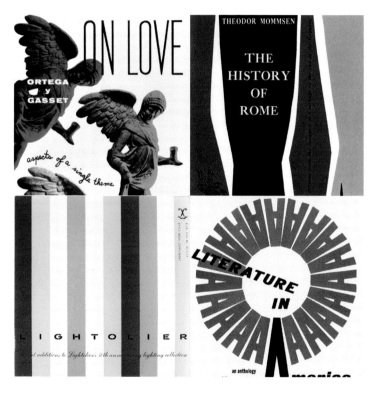

**Elaine Lustig Cohen**
**Modernism Reimagined**

BY AARIS SHERIN

GRAPHIC DESIGN ARCHIVES
CHAPBOOK SERIES: FIVE

RIT PRESS
90 Lomb Memorial Drive
Rochester, New York 14623-5604
*http://ritpress.rit.edu*

Unless otherwise credited, all illustrations are used with permission of the
Elaine Lustig Cohen Collection, Graphic Design Archives, Melbert B. Cary Jr.
Graphic Arts Collection, The Wallace Center, Rochester Institute of Technology.
Every reasonable effort has been made to contact copyright holders of materials
reproduced in this book.

FRONT COVER: Photo by Ugo Mulas
BACK COVER: Photo by Tamar Cohen

ISBN 978-1-939125-05-7 (PRINT), ISBN 978-1-939125-06-4 (E-BOOK)
PRINTED IN THE U.S.A.

**Library of Congress Cataloging-in-Publication Data**
Sherin, Aaris.
Elaine Lustig Cohen: modernism reimagined / Aaris Sherin.
    pages cm – (Graphic design archives chapbook series; 5)
Includes bibliographical references and index.
ISBN 978-1-939125-05-7 (alk. paper) – ISBN 978-1-939125-06-4 (e-book)
1. Cohen, Elaine Lustig, 1927–
2. Modernism (Art)–United States.
1. Cohen, Elaine Lustig, 1927- Works. Selections. II. Title.
    N6537.C583S54 2014
    709.2–DC23
                            2014017460

## Elaine Lustig Cohen

My life as an artist has been shaped by two passions: for graphic design created in the public sphere on the one hand, and by exploration of a related private vision in painting on the other. The book jackets and museum catalogs I designed in the 1950s and 1960s were intended to give the voice of the book primacy of place. In experimenting with abstraction, photography, and a playful use of conceptual ideas, I found solutions that were not being used in mainstream publishing or museum catalog design at the time. During this period I was also a pioneer in the field of architectural identification, creating new typefaces and signs for buildings by Philip Johnson and Eero Saarinen. In the last ten years, I have brought my worlds of design, photography, and painting together in a series of collage works on paper.

– Elaine Lustig Cohen

GRAPHIC DESIGN ARCHIVES CHAPBOOK SERIES

# ACKNOWLEDGMENTS

I was very fortunate to be able to meet with Elaine Lustig Cohen on numerous occasions in 2012 and 2013. Our conversations provided much of the source material for this essay. Elaine has an excellent memory, keeps meticulous records, and openly shared stories about her life and ideas about art and design making with me. Her sincerity and interest in passing information on to future generations is inspiring. This book is dedicated to Elaine in gratitude for her generous spirit.

The RIT Graphic Design Archive is the recipient of archival material on Elaine's life and work as a practicing designer. It was at RIT (Rochester Institute of Technology) that my own interest in design history was cemented, and I am grateful to Molly Cort and Kari Horowicz for introducing me to Elaine and inviting me to write this essay. Thanks to Professor Roger Remington for his work in creating the chapbook series and to David Pankow, former director of the RIT Press, for supporting this series and the continued acquisition of mid-century design archives. I am grateful to the RIT Press design and production team for transforming the manuscript into a readable book. And finally, thanks to Liz and Betty for providing constructive criticism and to Howard for his ongoing support of my work and occasional copyediting.

Aaris Sherin

**Elaine Lustig Cohen, 1972**
Self-portrait

# Elaine Lustig Cohen
## Modernism Reimagined

BY AARIS SHERIN

### Creative Impetus

"Making something is one of the most amazing things a person can do,"[1] asserted Elaine Lustig Cohen.[2] As the New York-based artist-designer pointed out, this impetus is uniquely human. Although she conceded that the desire to create is felt more strongly by some people than others, Elaine remembered that desire was always important in her own life. Elaine made a living as a designer during the 1950s and '60s, a time when few women worked in the field. Still more unusual, she worked as a freelancer, relying on personal connections and word of mouth to develop a robust client base. A consummate scavenger, Elaine used ordinary objects and original photos as the raw material for book covers and other client work. She has always been a collagist at heart, and it is choice and placement combined with the willingness to draw her own type and glyphs that gives her work originality and makes the images she uses feel relatable and familiar to viewers.

Elaine's career in design was cut short by a personal interest in exploring new media and a desire to realize her own vision rather than convey a client's message. In the last three decades of the twentieth century, she showed paintings, drawings, and collages at a number of New York galleries. Like many artists, she found that the drive to create is more basic and stronger than the desire to sell work or for public recognition. "It's almost enough for me

1 Elaine Lustig Cohen in discussion with the author, January 17, 2013.

2 Elaine Firstenberg took Alvin Lustig's last name when they married. Later, when she married Arthur Cohen, she simply added Cohen to her name and was known as Elaine Lustig Cohen. For the purpose of clarity in this essay, Elaine Lustig Cohen is referred to as "Elaine" and her husbands, Alvin Lustig and Arthur Cohen, are also referred to primarily by their first names.

**Elaine, 1966**
Photo by Ugo Mulas

3 Elaine Lustig Cohen in discussion with the author, December 10, 2013.

4 Elaine Lustig Cohen. A biography in recognition of her 2011 AIGA Medal written by Steve Heller. http://www.aiga.org/medalist-elainelustigcohen/.

to make something,"[3] she said, adding that she considered herself lucky to have been able to support herself financially while leading a life fully dedicated to creative endeavors. Elaine has been the recipient of numerous accolades and praise for her design and fine art. She was honored with a prestigious AIGA Medal for her contribution to design in 2011.

Writing for the commemoration for that award, critic and personal friend Steven Heller stated:

> Elaine Lustig Cohen is recognized for her body of design work integrating European avant-garde and modernist influences into a distinctly American, mid-century manner of typographic communication. Through Ex Libris (the rare-book dealership she ran with second husband Arthur Cohen), she became a fount of design history and a wise and generous resource for scholars and students of design. She is a living link between design's modernist past and its continually changing present.[4]

**Early Life**

Elaine Lustig Cohen was born Elaine Firstenberg in Jersey City, New Jersey, in 1927. Her mother, a native of Jersey City herself, married Elaine's father, who had immigrated to the U.S. from a small village outside Warsaw, Poland. Elaine's father, a plumber, initially moved his wife to Florida. However, after a hurricane hit Miami, Elaine's mother, who was pregnant at the time, insisted they return to Jersey City where they could be closer to family. Of the two, Elaine's mother was the more educated. She had attended high school and secretary school before marrying Elaine's father. A proto-feminist, Elaine's mother instilled the idea that being a woman wasn't a limitation. Her favorite line was,

5 *The Reminiscences of Elaine Lustig Cohen* (March 19, 2009), p. 6, in the Columbia Center for Oral History Collection (hereafter referenced as CCOHC).

6 Man Ray (born Emmanuel Radnitzky, 1890–1976) was an American surrealist and dada artist known primarily for painting, photography, and sculpture.

"You've got to do something with your life."[5] Because Elaine was the oldest of two daughters, her mother encouraged her to pursue her dreams; her parents supported various interests, including drawing classes, and later paid for her to go to college.

Elaine remembered high school in Jersey City as being unremarkable, but she was exposed to a bit of the contemporary art world through a friend, Naomi Savage, who was the niece of the artist Man Ray.[6] Proximity to New York City was also an influence early in Elaine's life. As a teenager and young adult, she was shy around people but more than made up for her public reticence with an adventurous spirit. Elaine would take the train to Manhattan for visits to the orthodontist and to explore galleries and museums. It was during one of these trips that she had the formative experience of visiting Peggy Guggenheim's gallery, called Art of This Century, which had a show of Kandinsky's work in an installation by Frederick Kiesler. Elaine found the exhibit remarkable and followed up on the experience with visits to the Museum of Modern Art, where she was particularly drawn to the work of Stuart Davis and Paul Klee. After graduating from high school, Elaine decided to attend Sophie Newcomb College at Tulane University in New Orleans, Louisiana.

**Elaine with her father and sister at the 1939 World's Fair**
Photograph by Elizabeth Firstenberg

### Journey South

Originally drawn by the warm weather and inexpensive tuition at Sophie Newcomb, Elaine studied art and registered for a basic design class taught in the style of the Bauhaus. After two years, Elaine's family moved to Southern California and she transferred to the University of Southern California, where she took painting classes and basic college courses, eventually graduating with a bachelor's degree in art. Though she was certainly committed to the arts from an early age, Elaine didn't remember ever wanting to be an artist in the formal sense of the word. "The idea of being an artist never even occurred to me," she remembered. "Coming from a middle-class Jewish family, I didn't know what it was to be an artist."[7] Above all, Elaine was practical. There were teachers in her mother's family, so becoming an art teacher made the most sense to her.

7 *The Reminiscences of Elaine Lustig Cohen* (March 19, 2009), p. 8, in the CCOHC.

8 The Modern Institute of Art was a short-lived art museum in Beverly Hills, California. It was only open for several years.

9 *The Reminiscences of Elaine Lustig Cohen* (March 19, 2009), p. 10, in CCOHC.

10 James Laughlin (1914–1997) was an American poet who founded New Directions Publishing. Laughlin hired Alvin Lustig to design numerous covers for New Directions books.

11 *The Reminiscences of Elaine Lustig Cohen* (March 19, 2009), p. 14, in the CCOHC

Elaine graduated from USC in 1948. After passing the exam to become an art teacher, she was given a post teaching in a junior high school for the following fall. With a job already in place and at her mother's suggestion, Elaine spent the summer volunteering at a new museum in Beverly Hills called the Modern Institute of Art.[8] It was there that Elaine met the designer Alvin Lustig, whom she would later marry after a brief but intense courtship.

**Alvin and Elaine**

Alvin and Elaine's first meeting took place during an opening at the Modern Institute of Art, where Elaine was a summer intern. The conversation was mundane, with Alvin commenting on the heat and a shy Elaine replying, "It must be the lights."[9] Later that evening, another man asked Elaine on a date and would later take her to a dinner party at which Alvin was also a guest. From then on, Alvin pursued Elaine almost relentlessly. Alvin's feelings for Elaine were clear from the start. In a letter written to the writer and publisher James Laughlin[10] two days after the couple met, Alvin stated he would marry Elaine. Alvin telephoned Elaine daily and asked her to marry him soon after. Elaine hadn't planned on marrying young, but she was overwhelmed by Alvin Lustig's attention and the intensity of his pursuit. Her mother, perhaps influenced by having married a man so different from herself, encouraged the relationship by repeatedly saying, "He speaks your language; what more do you want?"[11]

Alvin Lustig was already a well-known designer when Elaine met him in 1948. Born in Denver, Alvin had grown up in L.A. By the time the couple married, Alvin had designed New Classics book covers for the publisher New Directions. He had also been hired to create a think tank on design for *Look* magazine in

New York, where he met many of the most successful designers of the time. Elaine's life changed immediately when she married. Still committed to teaching, she spent her first year of marriage working at a junior high school in L.A. but found the experience less than rewarding.

The couple lived in a three-room penthouse on Sunset Boulevard that served as both living quarters and office. Alvin's life as a designer was infinitely more exciting than Elaine's as a teacher. "Every day I would leave the office where all these interesting things were going on and I would go off to these rotten kids,"[12] Elaine remembered. On weekends, Alvin and Elaine would visit with June Wayne[13] (printmaker and painter, 1918–2011), architect Richard Neutra,[14] designers Charles and Ray Eames,[15] the Arensbergs[16] (Walter Conrad and his wife Louisa), and other West Coast artists, designers, and intellectuals. During these casual meetings, Elaine's aesthetic sensibilities were stimulated. Teaching simply couldn't compete, and after a year Elaine quit and went to work in Alvin's office. Initially acting as a general office assistant, Elaine eventually learned the practical trade of design and production, creating paste-ups, arranging photo shoots, and readying designs for print.

**Move to New York**

In the late forties, Alvin Lustig was famous in the design community, but he wasn't making a lot of money. "Alvin had done a lot of work," Elaine explained, which included new titles for New Directions and designs for two buildings and the interiors of retail stores, but "nobody was paying."[17] Finances were tight because Alvin worked in less profitable areas of design rather than at an advertising agency or a magazine. By 1950, the couple was

12 *The Reminiscences of Elaine Lustig Cohen* (March 19, 2009), p. 14, in CCOHC.

13 June Claire Wayne (1918–2011) was an American printmaker, tapestry designer, painter, and educator who was born in Chicago but relocated to Southern California after World War II.

14 Richard Joseph Neutra (1892–1970) was an Austrian American modernist architect who lived and worked in Southern California.

15 Charles (1907–1978) and Ray (1912–1988) Eames were California-based American designers who were known primarily for their contributions to industrial design, modern architecture, furniture, and film.

16 Walter Conrad (1878–1954) and Louisa (born Mary Louise Stevens, 1879–1953) Arensberg were collectors of modern art based first in New York and later in Southern California. In addition to being a collector and patron, Walter Arensberg was a poet and critic.

17 *The Reminiscences of Elaine Lustig Cohen* (March 19, 2009), p. 15, in CCOHC.

selling their books to eat. When an invitation came from Josef Albers for Alvin to come and teach in a new program at Yale, Elaine and Alvin jumped at the chance to leave California and move to New York. The teaching salary from Yale and the money from designing covers for New Directions helped Alvin establish an office in New York, where he took on work designing interiors and building signage as well as completing more traditional graphic design projects. When asked about her contribution to Alvin's studio, Elaine was circumspect and pointed out that there were other support staff working in the office as well. "At first I didn't really do much," she stated. But eventually, through observation and firsthand experience, Elaine learned to do everything necessary to run a design studio. "It was like osmosis for me,"[18] she recalled.

18 *The Reminiscences of Elaine Lustig Cohen* (March 19, 2009), p. 16, in CCOHC.

**Elaine and Alvin Lustig**
**Los Angeles, 1949**

19 *The Reminiscences of Elaine Lustig Cohen* (March 19, 2009), p. 18, in CCOHC.

Alvin was born with type 1 diabetes, and in the early '50s his health began to deteriorate. As Alvin's sight worsened (a side effect of the disease), Elaine began to do more design work, though always with initial direction from Alvin. Additionally, after incorporating Alvin's aesthetic directions, Elaine would take the lead on interiors projects, including the design of several large Manhattan apartments. Elaine stated that there was no particular bias against her creating her own independently driven work. "None of the people in the office did anything original," she reported.[19] According to Elaine, she and the other staff worked to realize the aesthetic of Alvin's vision, meaning that the ideas for initial designs all originated with Alvin, and the other people in the office worked to produce the finished designs or products. This practice of a single designer being the starting point for all the work coming from a design studio or office was not uncommon at the time.

From 1952 until 1955 when Alvin died, his eyesight was increasingly compromised, to the point that he became legally blind. Rather than close his office, Alvin gave a party to announce that he was losing his sight but would continue to design. Working from his usual pencil sketches became impossible, but Alvin would verbally describe his ideas to Elaine and other employees working in the office. He used references from previous jobs for type, color, and materials specification. Although Elaine described herself as a mere "office slave" in Alvin's studio, her experience wasn't wholly different than that of contemporary junior designers. Producing the ideas of experienced designers is still a prerequisite stepping-stone for many young designers, and the concept and training are as applicable today as they were in earlier times.

**Elaine and Arthur A. Cohen**
**Mexico, 1956**

## On Her Own

In 1955, just before his fortieth birthday, Alvin died, leaving Elaine a twenty-eight-year-old widow with few means. Fortunately, some of the first calls Elaine received were offers of work. That same year, the architect Philip Johnson had commissioned Alvin to design the signage for the Seagram Building in New York. When he called with condolences he said, "Okay, Elaine, you do it."[20] Similarly, Arthur Cohen, publisher of Meridian Books, who had become a close friend and confidant of the couple, suggested that she design the book covers Alvin had originally been hired to produce. Even though she was terrified, Elaine was innately practical, and the fact that Alvin had left a mere $400 in the bank provided the impetus for her to become a practicing designer. While working with Alvin, Elaine did not initiate her own designs; but by 1955, she had built up considerable design and production experience. She knew the basics of how to make a mechanical and a paste-up and had supplemented her "on the job" training by sitting in on Joseph Albers's[21] lectures at Yale when she drove Alvin to New Haven to teach.

20 *The Reminiscences of Elaine Lustig Cohen* (March 19, 2009), p. 21, in CCOHC.

21 Josef Albers (1888–1976) was a German-born American artist and pioneering art educator. Albers was a professor at Yale from 1950–1958 and worked to build up the graphic design department by hiring fellow modernists Alvin Eisenmann, Alvin Lustig, and Herbert Matter.

As Elaine struggled to create a design business, she was once again being pursued by an ardent admirer. In addition to offering her work, Meridian Publisher Arthur Cohen had fallen in love with Elaine and called her. Nine months later, Elaine Lustig married Arthur Cohen. Elaine remembered those first years of working fondly: "I didn't work in the advertising field, but I wasn't making bad money compared to what Arthur was making at Meridian Books."[22] At Meridian, Arthur Cohen was creating a new type of publishing company, one that specialized in paperback books aimed at the college market. Up until that time, few companies had produced paperbacks, and the format was considered cheap and unprofitable. Arthur saw a demand and began reissuing existing titles on history, philosophy, and other subjects that students were required to read. Later, Arthur began commissioning original titles to be printed in paperback, and while Elaine ran a design office and designed covers for Meridian, Arthur Cohen developed a profitable business in publishing.

During the first years of their marriage, Elaine and Arthur lived in Manhattan and socialized with Upper West Side intellectuals who were friends of Arthur's. Elaine's flair for color and design extended to every facet of her life. Like her work on paying projects, her wardrobe was also an outlet of self-expression. She made the most of natural good looks, and she had an ability to choose clothing combinations that would attract notice. In the 1960s Elaine was thrown out of a fancy New York restaurant for wearing very short skirts, but being provocative wasn't Elaine's main goal. She loved the idea of "dressing," and clothing was simply a way of extending her creative reach.

22 *The Reminiscences of Elaine Lustig Cohen* (March 19, 2009), p. 22, in CCOHC.

**Living room of
Elaine and Arthur A. Cohen
New York, 1956**

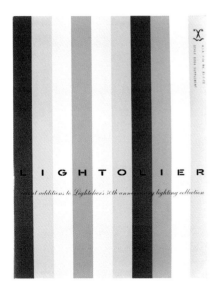

Lightolier
*Lightolier: recent additions to Lightolier's
50th anniversary lighting collection*
Advertising Brochure
1955

## Working in Design

As a designer, Elaine had many of the same types of clients that Alvin Lustig had worked with. She designed book covers and signage for buildings, worked with cultural institutions, created identities, and developed promotional materials for the 1964 World's Fair. Her two best clients were the Jewish Museum in New York and Arthur Cohen's publishing company, Meridian Books. Most of Elaine's work came through referrals. She developed signage systems for Philip Johnson and other architects and designed the interiors of homes and retail spaces. Elaine refuted any suggestion that she was hampered by her gender when working as a designer. As she saw it, "There were so few of us (women designers), the male designers couldn't have cared less about me. There were no freelance women around."[23] Since she didn't work for a company or an agency, Elaine was largely left to her own devices, and her work benefited from that freedom and flexibility. The broad range of projects she took on gave her the ability to experiment and try new ideas and different approaches to form making.

23 *The Reminiscences of Elaine Lustig Cohen*
(March 19, 2009), p. 36-37, in CCOHC.

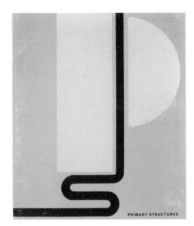

The Jewish Museum
*Primary Structures: Younger
American and British Sculptors*
Exhibition Catalog Cover
1966

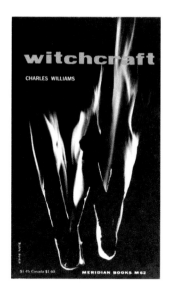

Elaine's sense of design was usually direct. She resisted using a specific format and never adopted a particular style. She also used the same approach for most of her design work, whether it entailed creating a catalogue for an art exhibit or designing the cover of a book for Meridian. Through the use of visual form, Elaine tried to distill the essence of the content. In some cases she generated compositions using abstract forms and type, while at other times she produced photographic compositions. Several Meridian covers look as though they were created using photo editing tools or effects found in programs like Adobe Photoshop. But the computer didn't exist when Elaine was working as a designer, and her techniques for image making were often remarkably simple.

Charles Williams
*Witchcraft*
Meridian Books
Book Cover
1958

# "A great book jacket never sold a dreadful book."[24]

24 Elaine Lustig Cohen in discussion with the author, March 4, 2013.

25 Photostat machines were early projection photocopiers used to make positive or negative copies of graphic matter.

Elaine was a consummate opportunist. Any material, technique, or color was fair game. She used the fireplace in her Manhattan townhouse to photograph burning pieces of wood for the 1958 Meridian title *Witchcraft*. Orange type overlays the black and white image; the composition is simple and immediately evocative. For the exhibit 2 Kinetic Sculptors at the Jewish museum, Elaine used type to convey movement. Often asked how she created the "blur" in the image several decades before design software became available, Elaine described pasting individual letterforms in a semicircle on white paper, setting the composition up in front of a Photostat[25] machine, and turning the paper. In the exposure, it appeared as though the type was moving in a circle.

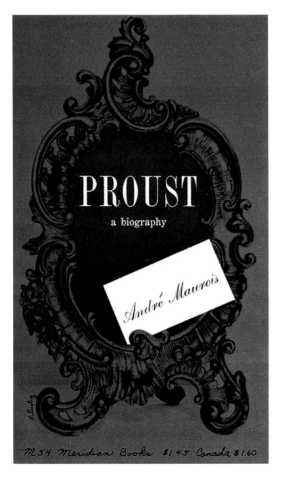

André Maurois
*Proust: A Biography*
Meridian Books
Book Cover
1957

Dwight Macdonald
*Memoirs of a Revolutionist*
Meridian Books
Book Cover
1958

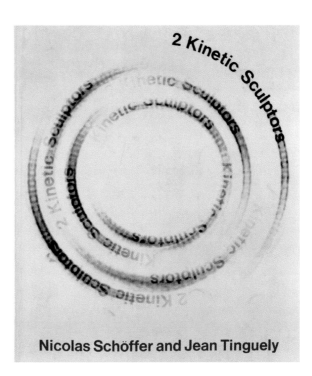

Saul Bellow, Keith Botsford, editors.
*The Noble Savage 4*
Meridian Books
Book Cover
1959

Nicolas Schoffer and Jean Tinguely
*2 Kinetic Sculptors*
The Jewish Museum
Exhibition Catalog Cover
1966

Elaine was constantly looking for and creating her own raw material. She took her own photos and used images photocopied from books and objects from around the house. For the cover of a 1957 Meridian book titled Proust, she photographed a picture frame she already owned and added a calling card she created. An image of a famous villa in Ravello, Italy, provided the basis for *The Noble Savage*, one of Elaine's best-known covers. An antique spike file served as the visual stand-in for the idea of a person taking notes in *Memoirs of a Revolutionist*. Overlays of blue and red and the addition of whimsical type enhanced the meaning of the image and produced a more fully realized composition.

While she never shied away from making the most of what was at hand, not all of Elaine's work relied on imagery or photographed objects. Some of her most successful covers use simple shapes and typography. What consistently makes these pieces stand out is Elaine's clever use of color and the placement of letterforms and words. The slight blur around the type in Yvor Winters's *On Modern Poets* gives the two-dimensional composition depth. A 1995 article in Eye Magazine described Elaine as "suggestively poetic" while at times "brilliantly blunt as in her choice of oversized bonbons for Tennessee Williams' *Hard Candy.*" Eye praised Elaine for using a variety of approaches, from "stark abstractions and concept-driven solutions to obtuse evocations"[26] and compared her work to that of contemporary book designers Chip Kidd and Barbara de Wilde.

The amount of time Elaine spent designing covers varied tremendously. Sometimes a solution would be obvious, while in other instances titles with conceptual or philosophically based content might require several iterations and a more nuanced approach. Elaine recalled working on *God and the Ways of Knowing*, which, she said "could be represented by nearly anything."[27] The content had no immediate visual associations, and she chose an approach based on color, shape, and type. First she bisected the composition with color; then she centered the type and the single visual element, a circle. Elaine kept the composition from relying too heavily on absolute symmetry by offsetting the author's name and adding a small dot to the right side of the circle.

26 Elaine Lustig Cohen. 8, 9. *Eye Magazine.* 1995.

27 Elaine Lustig Cohen in discussion with the author, March 4, 2013.

Tennessee Williams
*Hard Candy*
New Directions
Book Cover
1959
Reprinted by permission of
New Directions Publishing Corp.

Jean Daniélou
*God and the Ways of Knowing*
Meridian Books
Book Cover
1957

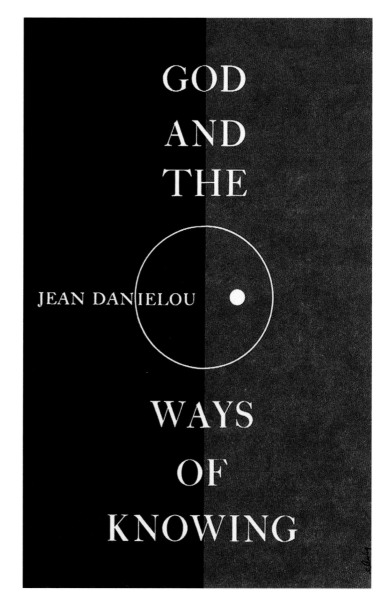

Theodor Mommsen, Dero A Saunders
John H Collins
*The History of Rome*
Meridian Books
Book Cover
1958

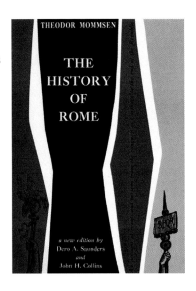

Justin O'Brien
*From The NRF*
Meridian Books
Book Cover
1959

Philip Rahv
*Literature in America:*
*An Anthology of Literary Criticism*
Meridian Books
Book Cover
1957

José Ortega y Gasset
*On Love: Aspects of a Single Theme*
Meridian Books
Book Cover
1957

Kate Simon
*New York Places & Pleasures*
Meridian Books
Book Cover
1958

28 Jasper Johns (b. 1930) is an American-born painter and printmaker.

29 Elaine Lustig Cohen in discussion with the author, March 4, 2013.

In the late 1950s and early 1960s, the Jewish Museum showed some of the most avant-garde artists of the time, and working with its director, Alan Solomon, provided Elaine with a unique opportunity. Solomon had the vision to take contemporary artists like Jasper Johns,[28] who had been shown only in galleries up until that point, and bring their work to a major museum. When describing their relationship, Elaine said, "I never had to explain my ideas to Alan because he understood what I was trying to do immediately and rarely disliked the solutions."[29] Similarly, being accountable to a single person (in this case Solomon) meant that she never had to present her ideas to a board whose members' taste might have been more fickle.

The Jewish Museum
*XXXIII International Biennial Exhibition of Art Venice*
Exhibition Catalog
1964

The Jewish Museum
*Max Ernst:
Sculpture and Recent Painting*
Exhibition Catalog
1966

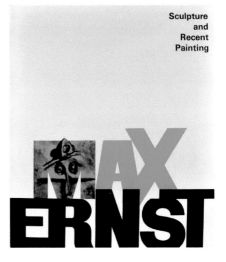

The Jewish Museum
*Kenneth Noland*
Exhibition Catalog
1965

Elaine emphasized how different her situation was from that of designers who worked in advertising or at magazines, where they would have to get concepts approved by sales and marketing departments as well as by the client. The projects Elaine took on were smaller, but her process was also more immediate. Having close friends and her husband as clients allowed Elaine greater creative freedom than she would have found had she gone to work as an employee at a company or a magazine. "Even for New Directions, the only one I had to satisfy was the man who gave me the commissions," Elaine said.[30] It was rare that an author would hate a cover, and Elaine remembered that, given the absence of undue constraints, design was fun. Creative independence didn't mean that Elaine adopted an "anything goes" attitude.

On the contrary, she was always careful to reflect the values of the institution or client and the particulars of the job.

30  Elaine Lustig Cohen in discussion with the author, March 4, 2013.

Tennessee Williams
*Baby Doll*
New Directions
Book Cover
1957

*New Directions in Prose and Poetry 16*
New Directions
Book Cover
1957

Tennessee Williams
*In The Winter of Cities*
New Directions
Book Cover
1957

Thomas Merton
*The Strange Islands*
New Directions
Book Cover
1957

All images on this spread reprinted by permission of
New Directions Publishing Corp.

## Typography

Elaine isn't known primarily as a type designer, but she did design a number of alphabets from scratch and used type to a greater or lesser degree depending on the needs of a project. She explained that drawing letters by hand allows a designer to have a special relationship with type, because "when you draw each letter separately, they will become your friends and get into your system in a way that doesn't happen when you just press a button on the computer."[31] In the late 1950s, the manufacturer of plaster letters gave Elaine the unusual assignment of cleaning up the design of some letters and designing a new alphabet. The letters were available in upper and lower case and were primarily used in display and exhibition design, where the shadows produced by the three-dimensional forms made them easy to read from a distance. Making the most of the project, Elaine repurposed her alphabet by photographing the letters in the form of the author's name and the title of the book when she created the cover for Yvor Winters's *On Modern Poets*.

When Elaine created signage for the General Motors campus designed by Eero Saarinen, she drew an entirely new alphabet. The type had to fit the architecture, and the resulting letterforms were kerned generously to mimic the low, spread-out nature of the buildings. Similarly, the signage she produced for the architect Philip Johnson needed to be subtle and not distract from Johnson's design. In her opinion, signage projects required a special finesse. The type was primarily informative and nearly always took a subordinate role to the more dramatic visual forms created by the building's architecture. When specifying components for signage projects, Elaine typically worked with the same materials as had been used in the construction of

31 Elaine Lustig Cohen in discussion with the author, March 4, 2013.

Yvor Winters
*On Modern Poets*
Meridian Books
Paperback Book Cover
1959

32  *The Reminiscences of Elaine Lustig Cohen*
(March 19, 2009), p. 50, in the CCOHC.

the buildings. "Today it is a very different field because many
people are doing this kind of work," she reported, but Elaine
remembered that in the fifties and sixties, "There weren't
many architects who were even interested in working with a
[graphic] designer."[32]

*General Motors Technical Center*
Detroit, Michigan
Signage
1957

Marca Relli
*Kootz Gallery*
Exhibition Announcement
1959

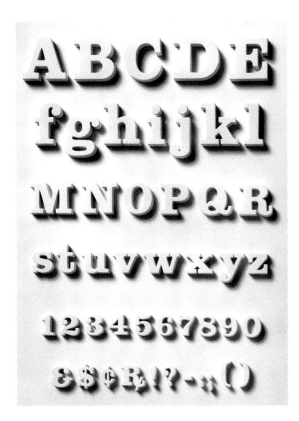

Mitten's Display Letters
Design of Plaster Letters
1958

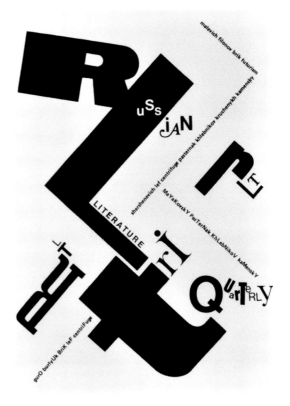

*Russian Literature Quarterly*
Ardis Publishers
Book Cover
1975

## By Any Means Possible

In the 1950s and early 1960s, many modernist fonts had only been developed recently and were marketed exclusively by companies in Europe. For Elaine and other U.S. based designers, these typefaces were highly sought after but often hard to come by. To solve this problem, designers would send for catalogs from German, Swiss, and English type foundries. As Elaine remembered it, "They would then painstakingly cut apart the letters and paste them together in a new order."[33] The resulting compositions would be reproduced as a negative by a Photostat[34] machine. The imperfections could be cleaned up with a ruling pen and black ink before the final plates were made. It wasn't long before European companies were able to get the new typefaces to printers in the United States, but during those first critical years, Elaine and other designers were willing to take on the extra handwork to use the most avant-garde fonts of the time.

33  Elaine Lustig Cohen in discussion with the author, March 4, 2013.

34  See footnote 25.

Arnold Toynbee
*Civilization on Trial and the World and the West*
Meridian Books
Book Cover
1958

Harold D. Lasswell
*Politics: Who Gets What, When, How*
Meridian Books
Book Cover
1958

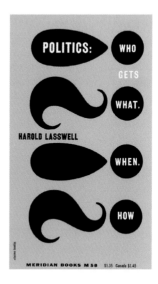

## Alphabet Studies

When Elaine learned to use a computer in the early 2000s, she was immediately drawn to the program Adobe Illustrator because it allowed her to create shapes from scratch. After decades of producing primarily paintings and collages, Elaine started to work with type again, this time creating alphabets on the computer. In her more recent work, letterforms are expressive and clearly have their own voice. Elaine is quick to point out that she doesn't actually "draw" on the computer but instead develops geometric forms from which she creates individual letterforms. She considers this new work to be "alphabet landscapes," and in them each letter is located as it would appear in the alphabet. The compositions are map-like and create collage of form. "They are about how color and collage can create a map of forms using the alphabet," Elaine said. She continued, "The alphabet is always fascinating. You fall in love with some letters and hate others."[35]

Stylistically, Elaine sees her alphabet studies as an opportunity to reflect specific ideas or historic periods of design. For instance, one alphabet is reminiscent of constructivists' work and was inspired by early paintings and drawn letterforms by Russian painter and theoretician Kazimir Severinovich Malevich (1879–1935).[36] Elaine's alphabet drawings use letterforms but shouldn't be seen as studies for usable fonts. Her alphabets are divorced from the specificity of content while at the same time leaving space for interpretation. The audience instinctively knows each form is a building block for language but is not burdened with an overt message.

35  Elaine Lustig Cohen in discussion with the author, March 4, 2013.

36  Kazimir Severinovich Malevich (1879–1935) was a Russian painter and theoretician who began by working in a modernist style and later was drawn to work with more abstract forms and geometry.

*Euclid*
Giclée print, 24 x 24 inches
2005

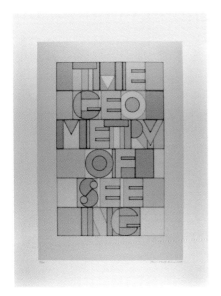

*Geometry of Seeing*
Computer print
21 x 14 inches
2011

*Homage to Malevich*
Giclée print
24 x 24 inches
2006

37  Elaine Lustig Cohen in discussion with the
    author, March 4, 2013.

38  IBID.

## Philosophy of Design

When asked about the difference between being an artist and being a designer, Elaine replied that each endeavor comes "with its own premise. With design you are always making a solution, whereas with painting you are forming the question." She continued, "As a designer you immediately have a space, a message, and you have to let people know what you are trying to say to them."[37] Elaine said she believes that the designer has to know what the parameters of a problem are and has responsibility to deliver a visual solution that is particular to that problem, regardless of the format a final design solution takes. "A designer should look at a problem holistically and design a solution that is particular to that situation," Elaine asserted.[38]

39 Elaine Lustig Cohen in discussion with the author, March 4, 2013.

40 IBID.

41 IBID.

42 Exit Art was a SoHo nonprofit gallery and performance space cofounded by Papo Colo and his wife Jeanette Ingberman in 1982. In 2002 the gallery moved to Hell's Kitchen. It closed in 2012.

43 Excerpt from catalog essay by Peter Frank for the 1985 solo exhibit of Elaine Lustig Cohen's work at the gallery Exit Art in New York.

### On the Openness of Modernism

Modernism is something completely personal for Elaine. She rejects any prescriptive rigidity and defined the movement simply as something different from what came before. "Modernism doesn't just cover one thing," she explained, adding, "I can draw from any period and I am influenced by painting, architecture, sculpture, and other forms of art."[39] For her, it is important to embrace variation. She said she would be "bored out of her mind" working with limited constraints in "a world so full of inspiration."[40] To prove her point, she offered Picasso and Miró as examples of modern artists whose visual explorations produced diverse bodies of work. Elaine added that even Josef Albers, who is most often associated with the square paintings, made other work as well. "I think modernism can be anything you want," Elaine offered. "It's just looking at something in a different way than someone looked at it in the past."[41] Elaine emphasized the lack of rigidity in her own work and said she would happily switch media, use new typefaces, and create work in different visual styles if the project should demand it. In an article about Elaine's paintings for the exhibit at Exit Art,[42] Peter Frank said, "Elaine Lustig Cohen maintains an awareness and fealty out of personal preference, not out of ideological compulsion." Frank's observation could just as easily apply to her design work as well; indeed, Steven Heller agreed, saying, "Elaine was not an ideological modernist but she favored clarity and simplicity, and used functional typography with asymmetry as a guiding principle."[43]

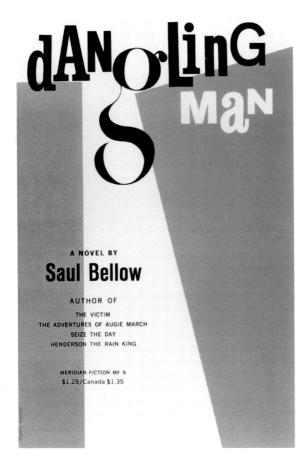

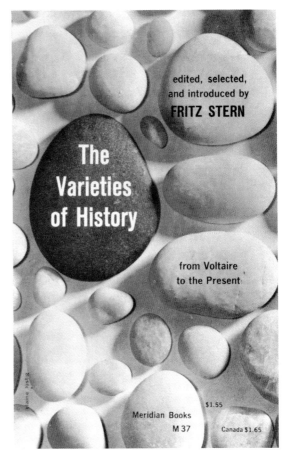

Saul Bellow
*Dangling Man*
Meridian Books
Book Cover
1959

Fritz Richard Stern
*The Varieties of History:*
*From Voltaire to the Present*
Meridian Books
Book Cover
1957

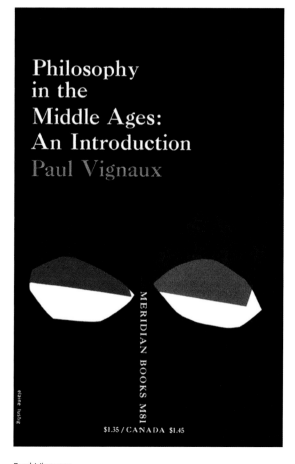

Donald Francis Tovey
*The Main Stream of Music
and Other Essays*
Meridian Books
Book Cover
1959

Paul Vignaux
*Philosophy in the Middle Ages:
An Introduction*
Meridian Books
Book Cover
1959

*"What is great about being an artist is that everything is open to you, if you want it to be."* [44]

44 Elaine Lustig Cohen in discussion with the author, January 17, 2013.

### Transition to Painting

In the late sixties, Elaine embarked on an uneasy transition into the world of fine art and painting. She was getting tired of working on the same type of design projects and, encouraged by her husband, Arthur Cohen, she began to explore new media. Even though her daughter Tamar (born 1960) was in school by that time, Elaine found it difficult to juggle the demands of home life while running a business. The realities of being a freelance designer influenced Elaine's decision to close the studio as well. Working alone or with a single assistant, Elaine couldn't take on large-scale projects. Instead, her clients were primarily arts organizations, museums, and publishers, and the projects had begun to feel repetitive.

In 1966, Elaine recalled, she went to great lengths to get a job for the FAA (Federal Aviation Administration) that would require her to redesign the signs and symbols used by the organization. At the time, she was working by herself out of a small rented office. When the referral for the FAA job came via the well-known art and architecture critic Aline Saarinen, she immediately

45 Elaine Lustig Cohen in discussion with the author, January 17, 2013, and *The Reminiscences of Elaine Lustig Cohen* (March 19, 2009), p. 55, in the CCOHC.

called friends to have them come and sit in the office so that her business appeared to be bigger and busier than a one-woman studio. In general, she recalled, "You didn't get big jobs, and I was getting kind of bored of doing book jackets and working with architects."[45] As the appeal of running a design studio began to wane, Elaine started to experiment with painting, a medium she had worked with at USC. The first show of Elaine's paintings took place in 1970 at the Johnny Myers gallery in New York. Over the next several decades she continued to exhibit work regularly in solo and group shows and was represented by Denise René, Mary Boone, Julie Saul, Pavel Zoubok, and other reputable galleries.

**Elaine, 1966**
Photo by Ugo Mulas

As an artist, Elaine was both ahead of her time and immune to the trends that characterized the art world during the latter half of the twentieth century. She was criticized for being a designer, a distinction that mattered in 1970 but seems quaintly passé today. "During those years, I would not admit to being a designer because if I did, I was snubbed," Elaine reported. She said the prejudice against designers is a thing of the past, adding, "What is interesting today is half the painters I know are designers as well."[46] Constructivist techniques and her early training in modernist principles consistently informed Elaine's work. During the years when abstract expressionism, pop art, and minimalism were in vogue, her work was distinctly out of step with what was considered fashionable. Elaine remembered not really being interested in movements like abstract expressionism and postulated that it was easier for her to come to painting through what she knew about design and her early training in Bauhaus principles with Alvin Lustig and Josef Albers.

Refusing to adhere to a particular style also set Elaine apart from other artists. She remembered how many painters in the 1970s and '80s produced bodies of work that varied little from year to year. For Elaine, such constraints, whether self-imposed or suggested by gallery dealers, would have been impossible to tolerate. Though Elaine certainly explored an idea or used a single media for multiple works, she had a general rule not to do a series of more than ten pieces. Recalling the transition from design to art, Elaine said it took her a long time to realize that what she was doing "was about form and not necessarily about design or painting."[47]

46  *The Reminiscences of Elaine Lustig Cohen* (March 19, 2009), p. 33, in the CCOHC.

47  Elaine Lustig Cohen in discussion with the author, January 17, 2013.

## Uneasy Relationship with Design

Though Elaine's paintings and later her mixed media collages were shown regularly, she never felt wholly part of the New York art scene, a fact that was underscored by the first major review of her first solo show. In it, the critic praised aspects of Elaine's work but also included the phrase, "but she's only a designer."[48] That criticism stuck, and Elaine began to distance herself from design, though she continued to take on the odd job and to design the catalogues for Ex Libris. Viewing it with the benefit of hindsight, Elaine continued to draw on the visual language of design, constructivism, and modernism. Writing for the catalogue of a one-person exhibit at Exit Art in 1985, critic Peter Frank discussed how Elaine was at home in the "constructivist mode," saying that she was one of a growing number of American and European artists who engaged in a "re-exploration of geometric-abstract tenets, with their positive—figuratively as well as literally 'constructive'—connotations." He continued:

> Unlike most contemporary artists–even the most fervid of post modernists–Cohen is willing, and even compelled, to declare her allegiances early, and to work within the parameters set by those allegiances towards a body of expression as heartfelt and consistent as it is vivacious, as fresh and surprising as it is familiar.[49]

## Ex Libris

In 1960, Arthur Cohen sold Meridian Books to World Publishing, and the couple was able to make the down payment on a townhouse on the Upper East Side of Manhattan and buy a Jaguar. Arthur Cohen went on to work as an editor, first with World Publishing and later at Holt, Rinehart and Winston, while still writing on the side. By the late 1960s, Arthur had left

48  Elaine Lustig Cohen in discussion with the author, January 17, 2013.

49  Excerpt from catalog essay by Peter Frank for the 1985 solo exhibit of Elaine Lustig Cohen's work at the gallery Exit Art in New York.

**Elaine in Italy, 1970**
Photo by Tamar Cohen

*Dada Rare Books & Documentary Literature*
Ex Libris
Catalog Cover
1978

*Lissitzsky & Maiakovskii*
Ex Libris
Catalog Cover
1979

*Russian Poets and Critics: 1960-1934*
*Avant-Garde Poetry & Formalist Criticism*
Ex Libris
Catalog Cover
1979

*60 Rare Periodicals*
Ex Libris
Catalog Cover
1978

Holt, Rinehart and Winston to concentrate on writing and scholarly work, and Elaine had stopped taking on design jobs to focus on painting. After several years the couple found they needed additional income. Both were interested in avant-garde ephemera and had collected some examples of early European modernism and design books. After successfully selling pieces from their own collection in 1973, Arthur and Elaine founded Ex Libris, and in doing so, became some of the first American dealers in European avant-garde materials. The business, which they ran out of their home, allowed Elaine to focus on painting and Arthur to write. The couple traveled to Europe several times a year to buy books and materials dealing with Futurism, Surrealism, Dada, Constructivism, and other atheistic movements of the early twentieth century. Elaine and Arthur often bought directly from an artist or from the artist's estate. They resold the items to collectors and institutional clients who were just beginning to build up their holdings of avant-garde books and ephemera.

In 1978, Ex Libris was moved to the ground floor of the Upper East Side Manhattan townhouse where the couple lived. Arthur was more involved in the business side of Ex Libris, and he did the research and selling. However, Ex Libris allowed Elaine to keep her hand in design. She was responsible for the design, photography, and mechanicals for catalogs (some of which are now collectable in their own right). Ex Libris provided the couple's primarily means of support until 1986, when Arthur Cohen died. Eventually, Elaine found that materials, which had once been so plentiful, were harder to find and cost more to buy, resulting in fewer profits when they were resold. Elaine closed Ex Libris in 1998, but she retained a large collection of avant-garde materials and continued to sell pieces occasionally.

*Catalogue of Catalogues*
Ex Libris
Catalog Cover
1982

*Russian Avant-Garde Rarities*
Ex Libris
Catalog Cover
1981

## Finding a Home with Mixed Media

In the late 1970s, Elaine began to work in mixed media and collage. The ability to combine found materials and self-initiated mark making allowed Elaine to unabashedly fuse her design sensibility with her skills as a painter and artist. Elaine continued her tradition of using what was on hand and collecting materials wherever she went. Arriving in Mallorca one summer, Elaine found the streets papered with campaign posters produced by local printers using woodblocks. The election was over, but the posters were still on the walls, and Elaine went out with a pail of water, a sponge, and a ladder and carefully took down and preserved the specimens for later use. "The posters were in primary colors with many different typefaces," she remembered.[50] Looking for another opportunity, Elaine "waited anxiously for the next election"[51] and rushed to Spain to look for posters, but she found that the twentieth century had descended on Spain and election posters used photographs of the candidates and looked like commercial advertising. "The new posters were terrible!" she recalled.[52]

Elaine's foraging was not limited to trips to Mallorca. She regularly visited flea markets in Europe and the United States, looking for source material for her work. Today, in her Manhattan studio, Elaine has boxes of ephemera that were too damaged to sell, finds from flea market crawls, and other materials she collected up on her travels. She doesn't hesitate to use rare or unusual objects. For one collage, she tore up a Dürer print. She quickly emphasized that the print was already in disrepair. Nor were items originally bought for Ex Libris off limits. Elaine said she's the only person who can rip up such valuable material.

50 *The Reminiscences of Elaine Lustig Cohen* (March 19, 2009), p. 69, in the CCOHC.

51 IBID.

52 Elaine Lustig Cohen in discussion with the author, January 17, 2013.

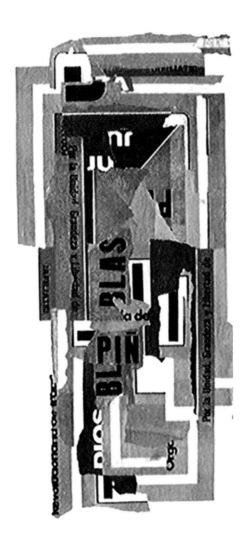

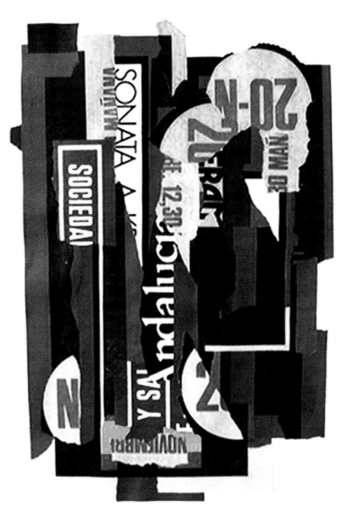

*Unidad*
Collage on Paper, 28½ x 17 inches
1979

*Granada*
Collage on Paper, 30 x 22 inches
1980

*"I think I've been about collage all my life. It's my language, so putting these forms together and cropping them seems so logical."*[53]

**Inspiration through Process**

For Elaine, inspiration may come directly through the process of making, but she is also stimulated by old photos, advertising, newspaper clippings, avant-garde design, and other material she has collected over the years. Vintage postcards of nude women Elaine purchased in Vienna formed the basis for a series of collages in the '90s. She said the postcards sat on her desk for a long time. Then, one day, she decided she wanted to tell their story. "I started to work on them and suddenly it became an obsession," she remembered.[54] First she painted directly on the images, and she later incorporated parts of images in collages and enlarged some images to change the scale of her work. Photography has also provided regular source material for Elaine. In Bubble Ready, a collage from 1999, Elaine used an image she took at the Kunsthistorisches Museum in Vienna. Another series from the early 2000s uses checkerboard patterns as an underlying structure. Elaine painted black and red squares on photographs and images from art history. In most of Elaine's collages, images are used as particular visual references. "If you're really a good art historian you would be able to identify each image,"[55] she said and pointed to the visual puns sometimes found in her work. "I'm only funny

53 Elaine Lustig Cohen in discussion with the author, January 17, 2013.

54 *The Reminiscences of Elaine Lustig Cohen* (March 19, 2009), p. 79, in the CCOHC.

55 IBID, p. 33.

*Sewing Box (edition 5)*
Lacquer on wood, chrome, velvet, pins, spools of thread
15 x 15 x 16 inches
1983

*Play It Xanti*
Photo with collage and acrylic
15 x 11¾ inches
1994

*Menschlichen Proportion*
Photo with collage and acrylic
15 11/16 x 11½ inches
1994

*Bubble Ready*
Photo with collage and watercolor
22¾ x 19 inches
1999

56 *The Reminiscences of Elaine Lustig Cohen*
(March 19, 2009), p. 81, in the CCOHC.

in relationship to something in the context of what's being said," she explained. "I don't come up with jokes, but I can be very pun-like or fun-like."[56] This observation was observation not lost on Steve Heller, who cited playfulness as an attribute of Elaine's in a 1995 i-D magazine article on her work.

Elaine was never particularly drawn to portraiture, but that changed in 2001 when the Museum of Modern Art (MOMA) in New York asked her to design a poster for an exhibit of architect

*Mies in Berlin*
Poster, 34 x 24½ inches
The Museum of Modern Art
2001

Mies van der Rohe's[57] early work. Elaine began by investigating the symbols of van der Rohe's life. She created a collage of photographs, images, and ephemera in which each piece had a specific meaning. She used an actual architectural plan designed by van der Rohe, an original 1922 map of Berlin, and a ticket from her box of Berlin flee market finds. The "G" prominently displayed in the composition references a 1924 magazine founded by Mies van der Rohe and Hans Richter called G (the full title was Material zur elementaren Gestaltung) and a cigar label from a box of cigars, all of which had illustrated pictures of architects on them. As has often been the case with Elaine's work, one project can inspire a new approach. After completing the Mies van der Rohe poster, Elaine created a series of 24 portraits of her favorite avant-garde artists of the 1920s. Each composition is a unique collage representing various facets of the designer's work and life. The series included collages dedicated to Kurt Schwitters, Theo van Doesburg, Piet Mondrian, Lyubov Popova, Tristan Tzara, John Heartfield, Hanna Höch, Alexander Rodchenko, Filippo Marinetti, and others. Of the resulting 2009 exhibit, *My Heroes: Portraits of the Avant-Garde* at Adler & Conkright Fine Art in New York, Professor and Design Historian Jeremy Aynsley wrote,

> The collages act as a collective homage. In no way are they pastiche. Instead they are full of the graphic wit, astute perception, subtle selection and reference of someone who has a deep knowledge of the principles of modernism. Each contains a portrait, derived from historical sources, which the viewer places in their own visual lexicon. An exercise of cut and paste, the collages become elegant essays on each chosen figure.[58]

57  The exhibit *Mies in Berlin* ran June 21–September 11, 2001, at the Museum of Modern Art in New York.

58  Text from the catalogue essay by Jeremy Aynsley for the solo exhibit *My Heroes: Portraits of the Avant-Garde* at Adler & Conkright Fine Art in New York. The exhibit of work by Elaine Lustig Cohen was on display October 10, 2009–November 14, 2009.

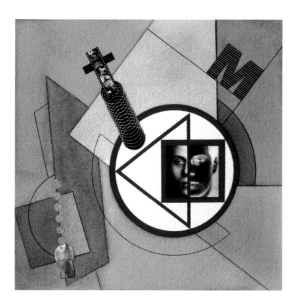

*Top left: Brancusi*
Collage and mixed media
16 x 16 inches
2009

*Top right: Hoch*
Collage and mixed media
16 x 16 inches
2008

*Bottom left: Moholy-Nagy*
Collage and mixed media
16 x 16 inches
2008

## Lifelong Relationships

As a young woman, Elaine displayed little of the self-assurance and personal strength that characterizes her older self. She credited Arthur Cohen with helping her to work on her confidence and said it was Arthur who pushed her to challenge herself professionally and artistically. Elaine acknowledged that her life would have been very different if Alvin Lustig hadn't died. "I would either have remained this shy, unproductive person or I would have grown up and divorced him," she said.[59] Like many talented artists and designers, Alvin Lustig could be self-centered and didn't always consider the needs of others. Still, Elaine is committed to ensuring that Alvin's contribution to design is remembered. She oversees the archive of his work at the Smithsonian's Archives of American Art as well as at the Graphic Design Archive at Rochester Institute of Technology. For decades, she has given interviews about Alvin Lustig. In 2010, she collaborated with author and personal friend Steven Heller to produce an exhaustive monograph devoted to Alvin's life and work.

Elaine may have "grown up" while being married to Arthur Cohen, but life with the intellectual publisher and author also had its ups and downs. Though emotionally generous, Arthur was prone to occasional bouts of depression. Artistic pursuits often took center stage for both of Elaine's husbands, and that meant tolerating less than perfect financial situations. Now in her mid-eighties, Elaine has been a widow for nearly 30 years, but she maintains very strong relationships with family and friends. She is very close to her daughter Tamar (who is also an artist) and stays in contact with a multitude of artists and designers. Not relegating herself to people her own age, Elaine has friends both young and old. Life has come full circle for her now, and the difficulty Elaine had as

59  *The Reminiscences of Elaine Lustig Cohen* (March 19, 2009), in the CCOHC.

a painter who was labeled a designer is no longer relevant. She continues to see herself hovering at the edge of the mainstream art world. There are many people who appreciate and have collected her work, but she isn't on major museum lists. She said, "I've lived at least three lives—all of which made me who I am today."[60] "In that sense, Elaine stated, "I have always been someone that people cannot easily categorize."[61]

### New Technology and Old Favorites

Many older designers reject new technology and continue to use traditional methods, but Elaine has embraced the computer as she believes it is a valuable tool, even though she is the first to admit that she is not that proficient with many of the programs and features of her Apple. Working with design software has allowed Elaine to create new work, but she still prefers to use original material and doesn't want to be known as a "computer person." She explained, "Now there are people who are really talented on the computer. But to me it always seems very mechanical."[62] She noted that she is troubled by the repetition of form sometimes produced by software programs.

Elaine continues to have a love affair with the tools she knows best, many of them ones she learned to use half a century ago in Alvin Lustig's studio. The ruling pen, ruler, X-Acto knife, compass, t-square, and scissors are her favorites. According to Elaine, there is something Zen about using a ruling pen; she suggested that young designers should experiment with one on days when they are bored with the computer. Elaine is gratified to find most of the tools she used when creating design work by hand are still readily available, something she worried about when the computer was first introduced. When asked whether she still

60 *The Reminiscences of Elaine Lustig Cohen* (March 19, 2009), p. 114, in the CCOHC.

61 Elaine Lustig Cohen in discussion with the author, January 17, 2013, and *The Reminiscences of Elaine Lustig Cohen* (March 19, 2009), p. 114, in the CCOHC.

62 *The Reminiscences of Elaine Lustig Cohen* (March 19, 2009), p. 85, in the CCOHC.

uses all of the materials from her early days as a designer, Elaine quickly pointed out that rubber cement no longer has a place on her desk. While effective for short-term adhesion, it doesn't hold up well with time, and Elaine still recalls how many old projects were ruined when the rubber cement failed and the projects literally fell apart in their boxes.

*ABC*
Watercolor and acrylic black ruling pen
10 x 10 inches
2007

**Conclusion**

In recent years, the design community has rediscovered Elaine and there has been renewed interest in her pioneering design work from the 1950s and '60s. She was awarded an AIGA Medal in 2011. In 2012, an exhibit titled *The Lustigs: A Cover Story, 1933–1961* opened at the College of Visual Arts Gallery in St. Paul, Minnesota. Elaine and Alvin each had numerous shows independently, but this was the first time their work was shown together, side by side. After a successful run in St. Paul, the show was moved to the AIGA Design Center Gallery in New York, where it proved to be one of the gallery's most popular exhibits.

It would be a mistake to presume to write a summation of Elaine's life or work, since she has never stopped working as an artist and occasional designer. Although she has not shown as much of her work as regularly as in the past, the product of recent years fills numerous flat files in her spotless home studio in New York. It now takes Elaine longer to create things by hand, and she finds it too difficult to work on large canvases. Nonetheless, she resists moving exclusively to the computer, saying that she comes from a different generation and values evidence of the artist's hand. Tomorrow, Elaine may unearth the building blocks for a new body of work from the boxes of ephemera that she keeps in her studio; she could begin creating a series of photos; or she may work with Adobe Illustrator and produce another whimsical alphabet. In the world inhabited by Elaine Lustig Cohen, technology changes, time passes, people move in and out of her life, but creative endeavors, regardless of media or purpose, remain constant.

**Elaine Lustig Cohen (2013)**
Self-portrait

| | |
|---|---|
| 1927 | Born Elaine Firstenberg (March 6, 1927) in Jersey City, New Jersey. She was the oldest daughter of Herman Firstenberg and Elizabeth Loeb Firstenberg. |
| 1942 | Visited an exhibit of Kandinksy at Peggy Guggenheim's gallery, "Art of This Century" in New York |
| 1944 | Enrolled in the Art Department of Sophie Newcomb College at Tulane University, New Orleans, Louisiana (1944-46) |
| 1946 | Transferred to University of Southern California |
| 1948 | Graduated with a bachelor of fine arts degree from University of Southern California (Los Angeles, California) |
| 1948 | Married Alvin Lustig. Began working in his office as a general assistant |
| 1951 | Move to New York after Alvin Lustig is invited to establish a graphic design program at Yale |
| 1953 | Alvin Lustig began losing his sight and started to rely on Elaine and other employees to complete projects |

| | |
|---|---|
| 1954 | Alvin Lustig almost totally blind and relied exclusively on others to complete projects |
| 1955 | Alvin Lustig died from complications of Type 1 Diabetes |
| 1955 | Elaine took over several design projects originally given to Alvin Lustig. She designed Seagram's building signage for architect Philip Johnson and book covers for Meridian Books. |
| 1956 | Operated her own design studio as a freelancer Aurther Cohen hired Elaine to design additional Meridian titles |
| 1956 | Married Arthur A. Cohen, Meridian publisher, author, and Jewish scholar |
| 1960 | Birth of daughter, Tamar |
| 1955-61 | Designed book covers for the publishing companies Meridian Books and New Directions |
| 1962 | Closed design office and worked primarily out of her home |
| 1963 | Designed catalogues and other collateral material for the Jewish Museum (from 1963–1968) |

| | |
|---|---|
| 1964 | Designed World's Fair graphics for architects Harrison and Abramovitz |
| 1969 | Stopped taking design work and began to focus on painting |
| 1970—1973 | Solo exhibitions of painting: John Bernard Meyers Gallery, New York |
| 1973 | Established the specialty bookstore Ex Libris with husband, Arthur Cohen. Continued to take occasional design clients and designed catalogs for Ex Libris |
| 1975 | Solo Exhibition: Galerie Denise René, New York |
| 1978 | Solo Exhibition: Galerie Carl van der Vort, Basel, Switzerland |
| 1979 | Solo Exhibition: Mary Boone Gallery, New York |
| 1980 | Solo Exhibition: Modernism Gallery, San Francisco and Janus Gallery, Los Angeles |
| 1981 | Solo exhibition: Nina Freudenheim Gallery, Buffalo, NY |
| 1982 | Solo exhibition: Carson Sapiro Gallery, Denver, CO, Gloria Luria Gallery, Bay Harbor Islands, Miami, FL Janus Gallery, Los Angeles, CA |
| 1985 | Solo exhibition: Exit Art, New York and Janus Gallery, Los Angeles |

| | |
|---|---|
| 1986 | Arthur Cohen died |
| 1995 | Solo show of painting at Julie Saul Gallery in New York Solo show of design work at the Cooper Hewitt National Design Museum |
| 1997, 1999, 2002 | Solo show of paintings at Julie Saul Gallery in New York |
| 1998 | Closed Ex Libris |
| 2001 | Designed the poster art for an exhibit of Mies van der Rohe's work, *Mies in Berlin*, at the Museum of Modern Art in New York |
| 2008 | Exhibited work at solo shows at Pavel Zoubok Gallery and Julie Saul Gallery in New York. The accompanying catalog, *The Geometry of Seeing: The Art of Elaine Lustig Cohen*, is produced<br><br>The Elaine Lustig Cohen collection was donated to RIT (Rochester Institute of Technology) Design Archives, Rochester, New York by Cohen's daughter, Tamar Cohen in October. |
| 2009 | Solo show at Adler & Conkright Fine Art Gallery (New York) with work inspired by 2001 collage of Mies van der Rohe. Exhibit title: *My Heroes: Portraits of the Avant-Garde* |

| | |
|---|---|
| 2011 | Awarded 2011 AIGA Medal |
| 2012 & 2013 | Exhibition of Alvin Lustig and Elaine Lustig Cohen's work opens at College of Visual Arts Gallery in St. Paul, Minnesota and at the AIGA National Design Center in New York |
| 2014 | *Elaine Lustig Cohen & Heman Chong: Correspondence(s)* was exhibited at P! Gallery in New York City |
| | *Elaine Lustig Cohen: Voice & Vision* exhibit opened at the Cary Graphic Arts Collection, Rochester Institute of Technology, Rochester, New York |

# COLOPHON

| | |
|---|---|
| Design | Bruce Ian Meader |
| Production | Lisa Mauro and Marnie Soom |
| Typefaces | Sabon designed by Jan Tschichold and Frutiger designed by Adrian Frutiger |
| Paper | Cover: 100# Blazer Silk Text: 80# Blazer Silk |
| Printing | Global Printing Alexandria, Virginia |